DOMINATE SALES:
18 CODES FOR SUCCESS

DOMINIQUE A. WILKINS

Dom1n8t Ventures

Copyright © 2017 by Dominique A. Wilkins

Published and distributed in the United States by Dom1n8t Ventures, LLC:
www.dom1n8tsales.com

All rights reserved. No part of this book may be reproduced by any mechanical, photographic, or electronic process, or in the form of a phonographic recording; nor may it be stored in a retrieval system, transmitted, or otherwise be copied for public or private use—other than for "fair use" as brief quotations embodied in articles and reviews– without prior written permission of the publisher.

1st edition, October 2017

Printed in the United States of America

I am the master of my fate
The captain of my soul
Here's to my ambition
The only thing to make me whole

My intellect and intuition
Turning Inspiration hot from cold

Cheers to my wins and losses
The bounty and the toll
They made me who I am
Quite fearless, very bold

Everyday I prove my value
I sell, I can't be sold

CONTENTS

INTRO		01
SECTION 1:	**PREPARATION**	03
SECTION 2:	**GREETING**	07
SECTION 3:	**DISCOVERY**	10
SECTION 4:	**PRESENTATION**	14
SECTION 5:	**OVERCOMING OBJECTIONS**	19
SECTION 6:	**CLOSING**	23
SECTION 7:	**BONUS**	26
AFTERWORD		29

INTRO

"Lord we know who we are, yet we know not what we may be"

\- JAY Z, "Marcy Me"

Like any great salesperson, I'd like to start with a question: *Why do salespeople exist?* Take a minute to ponder this query.

In my opinion, salespeople exist because human nature is to procrastinate. We naturally like to do things at the last minute. We usually don't make purchasing decisions when we *need* to do something. We take action when we *feel* like doing something. A myriad of excuses are created in the meantime. Therefore, salespeople exist in order to make the need so great, so important, that our prospects feel like taking action right now!

Notice the keywords: need and feel. The first rule of sales is if there is no need, there is no sale. The second rule is if there is no emotion, there is no sale. Think about times when you have purchased something, maybe car for example. You needed transportation, but your emotions push you to buy a Mercedes-Benz. Why is that?

You may have seen your favorite celebrity in one on social media. Your successful family member came to visit you and they drove one. Or, you saw how happy or successful the man in the commercial looked. That car has a certain emotional trigger because of what it represents: style, power, and success! That's how fulfilling your basic need, where a $10,000 used Toyota would fit perfectly, turns into a $40,000 purchase. It's amazing how strong emotions can be in fulfilling needs, isn't it?

According to the Bureau of Labor and Statistics, 11.2% of all occupations in America have a primary sales function. In my eyes, that number is really 100% because we all have to sell ourselves, our ideas, and our skills. We must be able to communicate our value and justify why we should be compensated. After all, in life, you do not get what you deserve. You get what you negotiate.

Dominate Sales: 18 Codes for Success is a discourse on a basic six step process that will help you unlock your sales ability. Learn to build so much emotion into your prospects needs that they will have to take action. Improve your ability to persuade and influence. Most importantly, gain the motivation and confidence that success can and will be yours.

Let's get ready to dominate!

SECTION ONE:

PREPARATION

> *"I take a plan, then I back-to-back it/ Hit after hit, check the batting average"*
> — Big Sean, "Moves"

I am sure you have heard the age old saying, "If you fail to plan, you plan to fail." The least successful salespeople are usually the ones who just "wing it." They do not conduct research or look for ways to improve. They are not curious or seek new information. The best salespeople, regardless of natural ability, are the ones who find every opportunity possible to grow. From reading random articles to honing their skills everyday, they are sponges and find success through the pursuit of being the best. This section identifies the three codes that need to be mastered before any sales conversation is had. Think of them as the warm-up before the game. By implementing these codes into your daily routine, you will only be planning for success.

CODE #1: It's Good to be Well, but Better to Be Well Rounded

We are all smart. At least in our own mind. However, brains are not the only qualification for success in sales. The most successful salespeople rely less on their intellect and more on their interpersonal or "people" skills. Ever met a salesperson that bored you to death with a long explanation of features and statistics for a certain product? Now compare that to a salesperson who seemed more interested in you and your needs, but gave you relevant information to make a decision. Which one is more likely to earn your business?

This goes back to an old adage in sales that says, "People buy from those that they like." People like individuals whom they have some common interest with, make them feel comfortable, and provide new insights or a new outlook. This adage rings true because everyone wants to buy, but no one likes to be sold. Forcing statistics and a list of features on the prospect only enhances their defenses. They will see us as just a robot who is trying to get their credit card. However, when we establish connection, we become a real person. This will make them more inclined to listen to us and hopefully feel some type of indebtedness. The only way to achieve this is to be well rounded in our knowledge of a wide range of subjects and people. Read several different publications relating to current events, sports, cultures, music, history, fashion, hobbies and your industry. Visit museums, art exhibits, festivals, and historic sites. Watch documentaries, short films, and Youtube clips. By expanding our understanding of the world, we are able to relate to all types of people in order to get them to like us. Our conversations become more like you're talking to a friend, than a transaction.

CODE #2: Know Your Product but Better Yet, Know Your Value

It goes without saying that we must become an expert in the product or idea we are selling. Keep in mind though that the technical aspects of the product only qualify our products or services to be of interest to the prospect. Those things are most likely listed on our website or marketing materials. There are probably several other vendors with similar products and services. So, why should the prospect do business with us? Therefore, it's more important to know the true value that our product provides. Does it reduce cost or increase revenues? Does it give a unique advantage? Does it give more peace of mind? Can we implement the solution faster? Knowing the answers to these questions and being able to communicate them is what turns our product or service into the best solution.

CODE #3: A Good Hunter Studies His Prey

The best attribute of any hunter is their ability to anticipate the habits of their prey. They know where to find it, what tactics to use to catch it, and what to do when things don't go as planned. The same goes for top salespeople. They are experts in the habits of the people who make up their target market. They know what aspect of their product or service is most appealing and why. They know what time is usually best to reach the prospect so that the conversation can be as engaging as possible. Most importantly, they know what objections are most common and how to overcome them. This information is then used to put themselves in the best position possible to make the sale.

Gather this information from past sales conversations. What worked and what didn't work? Why did you make your last sale? Why didn't the last three people purchase from you? When a tough question was asked, how did you react? By taking notes and decompressing after every sales interaction, we can put together a profile on customers, identify the common threads, and develop strategies to enhance the conversation. We will become more preemptive in the conversation and achieve success more often.

Lesson:

Sales success begins with being well-rounded, prepared, and practiced. In this information age, knowledge truly is power. Power to create connections and liking. Power to know and communicate the true value and distinct advantages. Power to anticipate obstacles and be steady in overcoming them. Gather as much of this power as possible so that you will be planning for success.

SECTION TWO:

GREETING

> *"If you want it, come get it, you know I stay super straight"*
> — Young Jeezy, "Put On"

In a sales interaction, non-verbal communication can be just as powerful as the words that are exchanged. The initial greeting is our best opportunity to gain an upper hand in the interaction by sending strong non-verbal signals about our stature, intelligence, professionalism, and demeanor. Without saying anything, the heart and mind of the prospect can be won over. At the same time, we have to be able to use all that we see to inform ourselves about the prospect. This will help us choose the best strategy to create liking and discuss value. These codes are for maximizing the impact of the Greeting.

CODE #4: First Impressions Make Lasting Impressions

When you meet or speak with someone for the first time, what are you thinking in the first 30 seconds? You're probably taking a glance at the other person's appearance and wardrobe. You may even notice their demeanor and disposition. In a sales interaction, this critical time frame is used by the prospect to determine if they want to do business with us. Have a clean and professional appearance. Give a firm handshake with a smile. Or if the interaction is over the phone, sound confident and professional. Be as warm and inviting as possible in order to begin the process of establishing familiarity.

CODE #5: See Everything as a Clue

As a great first impression is being made, also analyze the prospect to gain some insight into what type of person they may be. Are they in a good mood? Are they chatty or tacit? What kind of watch or jewelry are they wearing? Do their clothes look designer or bargain? All of these things can inform us about where the prospect places their value or how they make purchasing decisions. For example, the prospect may have on tattered sneakers but also has on a $1000 watch. He may also have on a wedding ring. We can gather from this quick visual inspection that he has above average purchasing power, but places value on items that are rare or hard to find. It can also be assumed that he is family oriented and, in a retail sales situation, he may have to speak with his wife before making a purchase. We now know that we have to make our product seem like a diamond in the rough and hard to attain to really gain his attention. We will also have to ask questions about his family and find out who the true decision maker might be. The purpose here is not to judge, but to use all the visual cues given to us to start to understand the type of person that we are dealing with.

CODE #6: A Strong Opening Makes Closing Easier

Now, it is time to get familiar. Give a compliment on that nice watch or suit jacket. Ask about their day or how their week is going. Find some common interests to discuss briefly. Focus on subjects that bring people together like music, sports, television, fashion, and family. Be sure to avoid divisive subjects like politics and religion as much as you can. Show the prospect early on that you are an authentic, empathetic, caring, and helpful person so that they can lower their defenses. Salespeople have garnered a bit of a negative connotation, so we want to separate ourselves from any bad experience they may have had in the past. Having an open, honest, and friendly conversation is what is most important and that is impossible without establishing a connection. Once the connection is made, the prospect is more willing to share critical information that can be used later on to close the sale. They will also be more willing to listen and trust the information they are receiving is accurate and honest. Otherwise, the conversation will become an unpleasant argument and ultimately a waste of time on both sides.

Lesson:

It is no secret that sales conversations can be uncomfortable for both parties. We are in the position of convincing someone that we just met minutes or hours ago to make a financial commitment to something that they are probably unfamiliar with. By mastering the art of making solid first impressions, becoming more aware of visual cues, and creating strong connections at the outset, the unfamiliarity and fear on both sides will disappear. That is when the real work of uncovering needs, presenting solutions, and closing the sale begins and will become easier to do well.

SECTION THREE:

DISCOVERY

"I sell ice in the winter / I'll sell fire in hell / I am a hustler baby / I'll sell water to a whale"
— JAY Z, "U Don't Know"

Having a great Discovery process is vital to success in sales interactions. Gaining a thorough understanding of the prospects true intentions and need is the goal here. This gives us vital information that we will need later on to close the sale. These codes give you the tools needed to get the most out of this important stage of the conversation.

CODE #7: Great Questions are Like Gold

Asking great questions is the most powerful skill a salesperson can display. They help us to get the answers we need to understand the prospects knowledge level of our product or service and what they may have tried in the past. We are able to confirm or re-evaluate assumptions that were made about their situation and uncover certain objections or concerns that would prevent them from purchasing. We can also determine what their budget or cost threshold is and know how fast they want to implement the solution.

Getting as much of this critical information as early as possible help to focus the conversation and deliver only the most important information that would be of interest to the prospect.

Questions also promote engagement. Great salespeople understand that you gain more success when there is a conversation and not just a great pitch. The more we talk, the less likely we are to have success because it is easier for the prospect to tune out and get distracted. Believe it or not you can, you can talk yourself out of a sale. When the prospect is answering questions, they are forced to give greater consideration to the conversation. They are also forced to make small decisions and commitments, leading them to mentally purchase the product or service before they even sign up.

CODE #8: Find the Need, Find the Sale

There is a *want* and there is a *need* that each prospect has. The want is the issue that brought the prospect to the market. The need is the true value that a solution has for the prospect. Most salespeople think they are one in the same, but elite salespeople know how to distinguish one from the other by asking great questions. For example, let's say you sell season ticket packages for a sports franchise. Every prospect you speak with obviously wants to go to the games. But, what purpose does coming to the game serve for them? Is it to spend more time with their family in an exciting atmosphere? Is it to impress friends or take out clients? Is it a gift for a loved one? Once the purpose behind the purchase is distinguished, go deeper with questioning in order to gather ammunition for making the presentation as effective as possible. Let's say that the prospect wanted season tickets to spend more time with family. Ask questions like, "What other activities have you tried in the past? Why do you think coming to the games would be the best way for you all to spend time together?

Who are the most enthusiastic sports fans in the family? Would you share your season tickets with others?" All of these questions invite the prospect to actively think about what this purchase will do for them, while giving you vital information that will be used to trigger an emotional response and gain leverage.

CODE #9: Nothing Happens Without Urgency

All prospects come into a sales conversation with some timeframe to make a purchasing decision. Most need to make a quick decision because they have procrastinated. Some are being proactive in an effort to find the best deal. Our job is to find out the urgency of the prospect as early as possible and work to make the timeframe for their purchasing decision today! The best way to create urgency is through scarcity.

People feel the need to buy things when there is less supply for fear of missing out. This could be scarcity of inventory, perceived discounts, or time. Once a deep understanding of the need is gained, start to create urgency around it as you move into your presentation. Continuing with our example of the family looking for season ticket packages, here is how this tactic could be used: "Sir thanks for sharing that information about wanting to spend more time with your family here at FedEx Field. It is amazing that you value family so much and we would love to help you create those lasting memories. <u>As you can imagine, thousands of families want to do the same, so inventory is moving quick for the best seats. But, let's get you the best available of what we have left.</u>"

Scarcity of inventory was created by showing the prospect that there is competition for fulfilling his need. Once the scarcity is created, become an ally.

The prospect should feel a little pressure to come to a decision quickly and look to us to help them get the best of the situation.

Lesson:

The Discovery stage is the best chance to take control of the rest of the conversation. Asking great questions to get the prospect engaged will help separate the want from the need. Familiarity built in the Greeting can be used to better understand the need by asking second and third level questions. Use this information to create urgency and speed up the prospects timeframe for purchase. Skipping this step could kill the rest of the conversation because it will not be personalized. It will become generic and more of an information session than a sales conversation. Execute this stage properly and the chances of getting the sale will increase.

SECTION FOUR:

PRESENTATION

"If we talking' bout money/ baby now we talking"
 - Lil Wayne, "Money On My Mind"

The Presentation or "Pitch" is the most glorified part of the sales conversation. It is what most salespeople focus on and practice because they think that you only need to be well versed in your product or service to get the deal. In actuality, the pitch is only as strong as the Greeting and Discovery stage. The connection and information gleaned from those two stages make it easier to personalize the solution, tell engaging stories that will captivate the prospect, and to discuss price with ease. These codes will help make your pitch great stand out from the competition.

CODE #10: Sell the Solution, Not the Product

It is easy to just talk about all the features of your product or service, but that is not enough to entice the prospect to purchase. Let's say that you are selling home security. There are over 13,000 companies in the United States that offer this service and they all provide different variations of alarm monitoring and sensors to get the job done. What will make your company special to the prospect looking to protect their family? Focusing on how nice the equipment is or that your company will call the police in an alarm event, will not create any differentiation between you and the next company on their list. However, if we focus on how aspects of the product are safer, more reliable, less expensive over time, and gives greater peace of mind, then we are onto something.

It is important to understand that this prospect is not solely looking for the physical product (the want). They are really looking for how much better the product is going to make them feel (the need). Let us consider another example. You are selling a premium SaaS (Software as a Service) product to corporations. Focusing on the technical aspects of the software will probably cause the prospect to cut the meeting short. Instead, discuss how the service can be implemented faster, how it reduces redundancy, and how the technical support team is available on call 24/7. This is more effective because executives are short on time and spend money on things that increase revenues, reduce costs, and provide greater convenience.

Remember, communicating the benefits the product provides and tailoring them to the deeper need is what will win the business.

CODE #11: Everyone Loves a Story

A great way to present the benefits of the product or service is to tell stories about how it has positively impacted customers in the past. Stories are extremely effective for 3 key reasons: engagement, social-proofing, and illustration. Similar to asking great questions, stories help the prospect have a greater level of interest in the conversation. Social-proofing is tapping into the phenomenon of social influence, where people mimic the actions of others. By explaining how others have benefitted, a subconscious seed is planted in the prospects mind which makes them think, "this person in my same situation had favorable results, so I will too." Lastly, we all love visual displays like pictures, movies, and infographics because they simplify a message. Stories illustrate the message of the total solution. Not only does the prospect hear the message, but the story allows them to visualize it and see themselves achieving the same positive outcome as the characters in the story.

A great sales story is comprised of three parts: the problem, the solution, and the outcome. Start by sharing the problem of past customers. Give quick details of how it was solved and finish with the outcome they achieved. Here's an example:

"Mr. Prospect, our product has a track record for success. I have a customer who shared a similar issue that you are facing. His business was facing the decision of upgrading their accounting software, but they were concerned with wasting their staff's time and resources to import the data and learn how to use it effectively. I was able to show him how our auto-sync feature reduces import time significantly and how our partnerships with banks would make payroll a breeze. This saved him the two weeks of training he thought he needed and allowed him to reduce his payroll expenses. He was able to save valuable time and money. I am confident that we can do the same for you sir."

Be mindful to keep stories succinct and impactful. Do not bore the prospect with too many extraneous details or effectiveness is lost. Be as ethical as possible and tell stories that are truthful. They do not have to be personal stories. The experiences of co-workers can be used as well. Elite salespeople are great storytellers. Become elite!

CODE #12: Price Ain't Nothing But a Number

Discussing price is probably the most uncomfortable part of any sales conversation. Money is always a touchy subject because prospects want the most value for the least cost. Everyone loves a discount right?! To dominate in sales, we have to be comfortable with the uncomfortable. Here are two things to remember to ease the tension: Always start with the most expensive product and leave room for negotiation. We give ourselves permission to assume the sale at or above full asking price because of how masterful the sales conversation was executed. We used the self-awareness attained during Preparation to establish a connection and liking in the Greeting. The Discovery uncovered everything needed to know about the prospect and his/her need while creating some light urgency. The Presentation was personalized with specific benefits and a story that illustrated the total value of the most expensive solution. At this point, we hope that the prospect is ready to pull out their checkbook or favorite credit card. Many will be, but most will ask for a discount. They are conditioned to expect it. More information is available at their disposal to compare prices and competition has ramped up in virtually every industry.

This has led to customers becoming accustomed to not paying full price.

However, there is a difference between a real discount and a perceived discount. Starting with the highest price creates a ceiling and forces them to either step up to the plate or ask about least expensive options, keeping us in control of the conversation. We should also build in a 10%-20% buffer above the actual price. If the product or service really costs $1000, pitch a $1200 price and gauge the reaction of the prospect. This gives us space to create a perceived discount during negotiations. Always leave room for negotiation because a sale is better than no sale. The negotiations do not always have to be around price. though. Negotiations can occur without lowering your price by becoming great at overcoming objections and reiterating value.

Lesson:

Impact is created from personalization, emotion, and aligning value with price. When you use all that you have learned about the prospect to tailor the solution to their specific need and tell engaging stories that force them to see themselves benefiting from it, it is easier to justify the price and have the biggest impact for both parties. Focus on the impact and the sale will find you.

SECTION FIVE:

OVERCOMING OBJECTIONS

"Failure is not an option, success is just a process"
— Wale, "Legendary"

Closing percentages (the number of sales divided by the number of leads given) vary from industry to industry and product to product. To some a 15-20% close rate is above average and to others, it would be below average. What is consistent across the board is that we are going to hear "no" more often than we hear "yes" in sales. Even if we had a 40% close rate, which is exceptional, we still heard no on 60% of our sales opportunities. As I like to tell my clients, "You don't get paid to hear yes. You get paid for all the no's you are going to take." So, a thick skin is needed in order to keep the conversation going after the first and even the fourth "no." These codes address the most dreaded part of a sales conversation: overcoming the objection.

CODE #13: "No" Means "Not Yet"

Even if we perfectly execute the Greeting through the Presentation stages, we are probably going to hear "no" a few times before earning the "yes" from the prospect. Their hesitation does not have anything to do with us in most cases. They may want to get several proposals to consider to make sure they are getting the best deal. Or, a negative experience in the past has them hesitant to make a decision on the first interaction. These are all legitimate excuses. But, they are just excuses and not a hard "No". They are a "Not yet." Remember, our job as salespeople is to inspire prospects to not procrastinate, so hang in there and find out what is stopping them from moving forward.

Start by confirming their understanding of the solution. Does it adequately fit their need? Can they see themselves using the product or service? Is there a competitor that they are comparing? Is the pricing comfortable for them? Are there other people who have a say in the decision? The answers to these questions will help to find out what the minor and major hurdles are. Minor hurdles can usually be explained away by reiterating a relevant feature or benefit that the prospect may have forgotten about. The two most common major hurdles are usually competitor research and price.

Isolate the major hurdle with a trial close. A trial close is a soft attempt at asking for the business and sounds similar to this: "I am glad that we cleared up some of the minor concerns you had and that we are a frontrunner in your mind. I can definitely appreciate you wanting to compare companies. It's just that time is the only commodity in this world that we cannot get back. So I want go above and beyond to save you as much of it as I can.

<u>If I was able to explain a few reasons why we stand out from the competition and it made sense for you, would we be able to earn your business today?"</u>

Isolating the major objection gives the opportunity to have a focused conversation on the only thing holding them back while gaining a commitment from the prospect. Following this up with another story and/or analogy to really drive home your point is another good way to go. While this tactic by no means guarantees a sale, it is a great way to extend the conversation and stay in the game.

CODE #14: No Bashing Allowed

There is a fine line that must walked when discussing competitors. Outright bashing other companies is unprofessional and will be a turnoff to the prospect. Shine a light on the best aspects of the product and service that are unique instead. Discuss the biggest competitive advantage and cite external sources as proof. Inform them of what they can only get from your solution and confirm that they see the value of those items. Point to the company's credibility through ratings, reviews, and awards and contrast with those of the competitor. Do your best to speak as if you are a friend trying to help them make an informed decision. This will gain more credibility and trust with the prospect. Here is an example: "Mr. Prospect, remember the auto sync feature we previously discussed. You said that you liked that it would save you time and valuable resources. <u>It turns out that we are the first company to actually offer it and our competitors still haven't added it.</u> Now, they aren't bad companies at all. But, we tend to innovate faster and our customers love how that innovation increases their return on investment with us. So we would be the best fit in terms of fitting all your current and future needs."

CODE #15: Save Your Best Card for Last

It is important in sales to be able to give up only the information that is pertinent to the current stage of the conversation. It is a terrible habit to discuss price or mentioning discounts during the Greeting for instance. The effectiveness would have been zapped away from that stage because they will only be focused on learning what the promotion is and not on making a connection. Overcoming objections is all about giving new information for the prospect to make a different decision. Hold back on talking about the promotion until you actually get a price objection. Save a couple of special product features that give a competitive advantage to use when overcoming a research objection. This way building value is extended past the first no.

Lesson:

It is natural for most prospects to create excuses and have legitimate concerns that prevent them from wanting to move forward on the initial interaction. After all, you are a stranger asking for their hard earned dollars after a short time period. This does not mean they cannot be convinced to turn that "no" to a "yes." All it takes is a little persistence. Explain away minor concerns and use trial closes to isolate major hurdles. Focus on differentiation, uniqueness, and specialization when discussing competitors. Hold some key information back about the product or service like special features or promotions and use it when necessary. This skill takes work to master but it will help improve production immediately.

SECTION SIX:

CLOSING

"I'mma win cause I'm too smart for these cats"
— Puff Daddy, "Victory"

Glen Garry Ross, a popular film about salesmen starring Alec Baldwin, popularized the sales acronym: ABC, which stands for "Always Be Closing." While the movie dramatizes the life of salespeople just a bit, it is spot on with the depiction of the importance of closing. These codes focus on three basic closing techniques to provide a foundation for more advanced tactics that can be adapted down the line.

CODE #16: Gimme the Business

The first rule to closing is to ask for the business! Almost half of all sales calls end without an attempt to close the sale. Time and energy has already been invested into the conversation, so make it worth it. An easy way to ask for the sale in a very comfortable and natural way is to assume it. After overcoming the objections, start to gather the pertinent information needed to finalize the transaction. Ask questions like, "Where would you like the product shipped and when do you want it to arrive?" Or, "What is the full name on the credit or debit card that you would like to use?" When done smoothly and confidently, the prospect will proceed without hesitation because the work of earning the sale has already been done.

CODE #17: Option Your Way to Yes

One of the most effective closing techniques is the option close. People like options because it gives them the feeling of having more power over their decision. If I were to ask you, "What kind of pizza do you want?", you are probably going to say, "I don't know. What are my options?" Now if I were to ask, "Do you want pepperoni or cheese pizza?", you would be more inclined to give me a direct answer. The same principle applies to sales. Give the option between the most expensive solution and a lesser expensive solution. Or explain the pros of choosing the solution today versus the cons of waiting a week. This helps to make sure that you sell something more often.

CODE #18: Sometimes You Have to Sell the Fear

While benefit selling should be the go to strategy, there will also come a time to sell the fear of indecisiveness. There are prospects out there that will give buying signs throughout the entire conversation, then give a myriad of objections to overcome. They will negotiate tooth and nail for every available discount and then decide to hold off on making a decision. This is typically the best time to use this tactic. It is usually executed by placing a "today only" contingency on the incentives that were secured for them.

An example of this might be, "Mr. Prospect, I have enjoyed our conversation today and you are definitely a great negotiator. <u>But I'm only able to secure these incentives today because I was able to get something approved that we do not usually do.</u> You have confirmed with me that we fit all of your needs and that the solution makes sense. So, let's go ahead and get you started today."

This communicates the seriousness of the situation and challenges them to make the decision now.

This tactic can also be executed by taking away the solution altogether and communicate the pros of moving forward now versus the cons of procrastinating or choosing a competitor. For example, "<u>Mr. Prospect, respectfully, everyone is not a good fit for our product.</u> I really think you are because you loved the features we have discussed and understood how we stand out from our competitors. Of course, you can choose whomever you want, but doesn't it make sense to go with the best company that fits your needs even if it is a little more of an investment? Why choose a cheaper option that will really end up being more expensive over time because they aren't a total solution?" When resorting to this tactic, make sure that your tone is not condescending. Stay professional and warm to give the impression that you are trying to work in their best interest.

Lesson:

A salesperson is only valuable when making sales. In order to make sales, know how to close. It can be uncomfortable at times and unnerving, but stick to your guns and ask for the sale. Whether assuming the sale, going with the options, trying the takeaway, or implementing all three, be sure to keep the customer first and communicate a warm and caring tone. Remember your ABC's: Always Be Closing!

SECTION SEVEN:

BONUS

Increasing Your Sales Production

Here are a few bonus codes that will help multiply the work that you have already done with a prospect turned customer. Sales conversations can be emotional, intense, and time consuming, so make the most of the time that you have invested.

CODE #19: Pipeline

Not every sales conversation will end favorably on the initial interaction. Sometimes the prospect is not qualified, just not ready to make a decision, or has an objection that cannot be overcome at that point and time. And that is okay. The more people you have great conversations with, the more sales you will attain.

Even if they come through at a later time. If the prospect shows genuine interest and you feel confident that they could eventually purchase, it is best to continue to follow up with them at an interval that matches their situation. Check in with a phone call or email. According to the Brevet Group, 80% of all sales requires at least 5 follow up calls after initial contact. 44% of sales reps give up after 1 follow up call. The extra effort is worth the reward.

CODE #20: Grace Them to Loyalty

Customer retention and upselling is one of the best ways to put more money in your pocket as a salesperson. This customer is already familiar with you and trusts your product, so why wouldn't they buy more of it? Be sure to continue to nurture the relationship after the sell. Send them an article about a topic you may have discussed. Give them a call on their birthday. When leads get low or you are having a tough time closing new business, that upsell could make all of the difference.

CODE #21: 1 + 1 = 3

Another great way to increase earnings or save a bad sales month is to actively seek out referrals. 91% of customers say that they would give referrals, but only 11% of sales reps ask for them. Moreover, the sales reps who do ask for referrals earn 4 to 5 times more than those who do not. Again, the work of earning trust is already done with your customer. They have friends, family, and co-workers who may need the solution as well. Even in the digital age, word of mouth is still the best form of marketing!

CONCLUSION:

Success in sales has less to do with the actual product or service we represent and more to do with our personal ability to use benefits and emotions to create total solutions. By employing a structured sales process, like the one outlined by these codes, we are able to do so more accurately and consistently. We will earn greater confidence from being prepared and practiced, which will lead to our increased success. Now that you have the codes, what will you do with them? What purpose can you fulfill with the new insight that you have? Ask yourself these questions, set your course, and go dominate!

AFTERWORD

I hope you have enjoyed reading this discourse as much as I enjoyed writing it. I have dedicated my intellect, talents, and several thousand hours to the sales profession over the last ten years. It has helped me improve my position in life, gain some influence in the corporate world, and allowed me to meet and learn from individuals of every walk of life. This is the culmination of my experiences thus far and I pray that it grows wings, lifting me to a higher level of impact. Take what you need and revisit as necessary to continue your growth toward consistent success. We are all salespeople in this new, globalized society made smaller by social media. Your personal brand is more important than ever. Your success will be dependent upon your ability to create connection, find needs to be met, communicate your value, overcome oppressive objections, and close the deals that bring your dreams to life.

I would love to hear stories of triumph or your feedback on the material. Feel free to email me at dw@dom1n8tsales.com.

Wishing you peace and blessings, your sales coach,

Dom

www.ingramcontent.com/pod-product-compliance
Lightning Source LLC
Chambersburg PA
CBHW050251230526
45470CB00005B/2206